Five Steps to Living

Your

Dream

How to Build Your Life the Right Way

Miriam Jones

REALLY**EDUCATED**

REALLY**EDUCATED**

www.reallyeducated.com

ISBN: 979-8-9880973-3-4 (paperback)

979-8-9880973-2-7 (e-book)

DEDICATION

This one is for the dreamers. The ones who lay awake at night knowing that they have something special to share. The ones with vision, passion, and purpose. This one is for you.

Table of Contents

"What Is Your Dream, and Why Is It So Important?"

What is your dream? You know, the thing that has been on your mind, the thing you love, the one thing that you know would make your life better forever.

We all have a dream that we wish we could accomplish, but secretly don't know how to start. I have great news for you, today that changes. That's right, you've made the decision to look for answers, and I am here to help.

This book will give you five foundational principles to build your dream so that you can live the life you've imagined. Dreamers make the world go around. They are the creators, the problem solvers, the leaders, and the winners. That includes you.

A word of warning, it will take work. Every day will not be easy and living your dream requires commitment, courage, and dedication. Only proceed if you are ready and willing to do so (and I know you are)!

With that said, let's get started on this journey of turning your vision into a reality.

What to Expect

This book is formatted to make it as easy as possible for you to get started. Each chapter provides helpful information and some practical assignments for you to complete. As you do, you will find day by day your vision will grow and your ability to put it all into action will increase. You are encouraged to keep a journal and complete each task before moving on to the next section. Doing so will help you to keep track of your progress and adjust accordingly.

CHAPTER ONE

The Blueprint

Step One: Develop Your Vision

The first step in building the life you want is to figure out your expectations. What is it that you want to get out of each day? What is your vision for the future?

Finding Your Dream

One way to begin to develop this picture is to create a vision board. You can use pictures from magazines or go online and compile images that represent the type of lifestyle that you wish to live. Having a visual indication of where you want to go will help you to remain focused on what is important to you.

Developing Your Vision

Another way to begin figuring out the direction that you would like to take is to look inward. What do you enjoy about your life? What are your hobbies? What is your passion? By knowing what inspires you, it will become easier to go about fulfilling your goals in a way that naturally connects with who you are.

Imagine wanting to build your own home. First, you would look at model homes, locate an area to build, and research costs. The same idea applies to building your dream. Before you can achieve it, you need a vision. Your vision is developed and supported by research and your natural abilities.

Once you understand your goals, passion, skills, and preferences, you can create a concrete plan. This is your blueprint, and what you will follow as you begin to lay the foundation.

DREAM BUILDING PRINCIPLE:

Before you can achieve your dream, you must have a vision. Your vision is developed and supported by research and your unique internal makeup.

DREAM BUILDERS ACTION PLAN

1. Make a list of your top three skills. Write out how each will play a role in making your dream come to life.

2. Create a vision board that contains every element of the life that you desire. Post the board up on your wall or save it as a

screensaver. Look at it daily as a reminder of where you are headed.

3. Write down a personal vision statement. This is a couple of sentences that describes who you are and where you see yourself in the future.

4. For the next week, take 30 minutes each day to research whatever industry your dream is in.

CHAPTER TWO

The Foundation

Step Two: Create a Secure Environment

Now that you have developed a blueprint for your journey, it is time to begin breaking ground. Taking action is what turns your dream from a wish to a work in progress. Having a strong base is what will give you balance as you move forward.

Finding the Right People

In life, think of your foundation as the people who hold you up, the individuals that surround you. Having too few connections will make carrying the load much more difficult than it needs to be. Therefore, it is important to engage with people who have your best interest at heart. They will provide the backing you need when things get difficult.

You also want to make sure that you find supporters who share the same goals and passions as you, including individuals that can provide guidance and professional insight.

Creating Your Framework

Once you have determined who is accompanying you on the journey, it is time to begin putting up the framework. This means creating a systematic way of doing things. Generally, this includes implementing a schedule to ensure that tasks that need to be completed get done, and that your time is allocated wisely.

Having a good system in place allows you to be more productive because it takes the pressure off trying to figure out what to do next or wasting energy on the wrong things. The less you have to think, the more space you'll have to enjoy life, be creative, and perform income generating activities.

From a business perspective, some systems you may want to consider are email, file storage, calendaring, scheduling, task and project management, accounting, content creation, marketing, website design and development, banking and merchant account set up, order processing, and client management. These are just a few options, and depending on the business, your needs may vary.

Taking Action

Just as important as having a reliable network of people to support you, is the consideration of who will help you carry out your mission. Leveraging other people's talents is a great way to reach your goals quicker while maintaining flexibility and freedom. Vision plus action equals success. Taking action requires a sacrifice of time, money, or control. If you are short on money, then you will need to invest more time. Similarly, if you are short on time but have the money, then it may be worth it to pay someone to help you. If you want to do things yourself and are unwilling to sacrifice control, it will cost you time. Whatever path you choose, just know there will be a tradeoff.

DREAM BUILDING PRINCIPLE:

Having the right people and systems in place will make doing things much easier and frees up time for you to focus on what matters the most.

DREAM BUILDERS ACTION PLAN

1. Make a list of the people who will support you on your journey. Divide the list into friends, family, business partners, and mentors.

2. Reach out to each person on your list at least once a month.

3. Create a daily schedule. Be sure to block out time for the following: money making activities, family time, personal time, sleep, knowledge building, spiritual/reflection, and household tasks.

4. Research apps and software that can help streamline your tasks. Begin analyzing and implementing those systems.

Sample Daily Schedule

Wake Up

7:00 a.m. - 7:30 a.m.

Spiritual/Reflection

7:30 a.m. - 8:00 a.m.

Breakfast

8:00 a.m. - 8:30 a.m.

Exercise

8:30 a.m. - 9:00 a.m.

Shower

9:00 a.m. - 9:30 a.m.

Knowledge Building

9:30 a.m. - 10:30 a.m.

Money Making Activity

10:30 a.m. - noon

Lunch

noon - 1:00 p.m.

Household Tasks

1:00 p.m. - 1:30 p.m.

Money Making Activity

1:30 p.m. - 3:00 p.m.

Family Time

3:00 p.m. - 6:00 p.m.

Dinner

6:00 p.m. - 7:00 p.m.

Family Time/Household Tasks

7:00 p.m. - 8:30 p.m.

Personal Time

8:30 p.m. - 9:30 p.m.

Money Making Activity

9:30 p.m. - 10:30 p.m.

Spiritual/Reflection

10:30 p.m. - 10:45 p.m.

Sleep

10:45 p.m.

CHAPTER THREE

The Interior

Step Three: Discover Your Identity and Protect Your Assets

You've begun building on a solid foundation and are surrounded by a community of supporters. Your systems are in place, and now it is time to begin putting up the walls.

Creating Tangible Evidence of Your Vision

Developing your product or service involves doing research, brainstorming ideas, and creating your identity. This is how you want the world to view you. During this phase some questions you want to consider are: How will you dress, speak, and interact with others? What makes you different? How will you help people and what products, or services will you provide? What will your business structure be?

All of these elements are important. This is also the part where you really get to craft your ideas in a way that fits who you are. Consider working with a graphic designer to help with branding, packaging, and other product related needs.

Protecting Your Investment

Once you have figured out what you will provide, to whom, how, where, and for what price, it would be a good idea to begin thinking about how you will protect your dream from being stolen. This safeguard can come in many forms including legally incorporating your business, filing a trademark, copyright, or patent, investing in insurance, creating trusts, estate planning, developing terms of service, contracts, privacy policies, and refund procedures. It is always best to seek the advice of a professional such as an attorney, accountant, or real estate agent for a thorough explanation of these issues.

Something else to be cautious of are dream killers. These are individuals that can try to interfere with your progress by injecting negativity, fear, or doubt into your life. It is very important to guard your mind and body from these types of attacks.

Make sure that you are filling your mind with positivity daily. This can be done by reading, listening to music, relaxing, and centering your energy through prayer, exercise, and quiet time. Success stems from having a positive internal balance, so be sure to keep yourself in alignment as much as possible.

DREAM BUILDING PRINCIPLE:

Protect your dream by seeking professional advice in areas that you do not understand.

DREAM BUILDERS ACTION PLAN

1. Write down what product or service you plan to offer.

2. List three ways that you will protect yourself against dream stealers.

3. Make a list of your strengths and weaknesses. How will you use your strengths and improve your weaknesses to further your progress?

4. Contact an attorney, accountant, or graphic designer this week to discuss any concerns you may have.

Guard your mind, guard your heart. Protect your vision from the start.

CHAPTER FOUR

The Exterior

Step Four: Engage and Make Connections

You have the internal structure of your life together, now it's time to begin working on the external. This is the way you present yourself to the world.

Managing Your Image

Marketing is everywhere. The way that you carry yourself can speak volumes. Take this opportunity to think about the image that you are projecting each time you walk out of the house. The goal is to be true to yourself and the dream you have. You will attract like-minded individuals by the energy you give off. Be sure that you are walking in authenticity, otherwise you may end up attracting the opposite of what you intend.

Marketing and Making Connections

From a business perspective, marketing simply involves making the world aware of what you have to offer. You could have the greatest service or idea, but if no one knows about it, then it is likely you will not be as successful as you could be. It does not have to be complicated.

Think of ways that you can share your offerings with the world that you are comfortable doing. If you do not like social media and prefer in person interactions, then try to find local events that you can attend that relate to your area of interest. Wear a company shirt, rent a booth, strike up conversation with other people at the function and make new connections.

Maybe you are not a people person. In that case, look into creating flyers or mailers to distribute, create a blog, or hire someone to run paid advertisements for you. Be creative and keep it simple. There are all types of promotional products that can be used as giveaways such as water bottles, t-shirts, magnets, and pens. The point is simply to let as many people as possible know about who you are and what you do.

DREAM BUILDING PRINCIPLE:

The more authentic you are in the way you present yourself to the world, the easier it is to attract the right type of people to participate in your vision.

DREAM BUILDERS ACTION PLAN

1. Make a list of ways that you can use marketing to help others become aware of your dream.

2. Describe your ideal "tribe" or customer. What do they look like? What do they enjoy? Where do they live? Why would they want or need your service or product?

3. Attend one event or conference in your area this month.

4. Enroll in an online marketing course. Take what you learn and implement it into making your dream a reality.

The more lives you touch, the quicker your dream can grow.

CHAPTER FIVE

The Walkthrough

Step Five: Reflect and Refine

Congratulations, you have made it to the final step. Along the way you have solidified your vision, surrounded yourself with the right people, put systems into place, sought professional advice, and begun marketing. Now it's time to take a moment to fine tune your processes and adjust as needed.

Inspections and Adjustments

Fulfilling your dream is a lifelong journey. As you have learned, it requires a lot of groundwork to get started. The good news is, once the initial heavy lifting is done, the focus shifts from building to management. Your role now is to analyze the areas of your plan that are working and the ones that are not. Look for opportunities to grow and improve your skills and offerings.

Some things to keep an eye on are your finances, where you are spending most of your money, taxes, income, costs, effectiveness of marketing initiatives, time management, project management, scheduling, and labor if applicable. As you continue to grow, your environment may change. Just like the seasons, new people and opportunities will come your way while old relationships and doors may close. The key is to remain grounded and focused on the infrastructure that you have built to weather the storm.

DREAM BUILDING PRINCIPLE:

Ongoing maintenance and management are necessary to ensure the longevity of your success.

DREAM BUILDERS ACTION PLAN

1. Take some time this week to analyze your progress. What improvements can be made?

2. Make a list of your top trouble areas. What needs to be done to address these issues?

3. Based on your current situation, write down three goals that you would like to complete by next year and how you will do so.

4. List one growth opportunity that you have. Focus on exploring this option for the next six months.

Things to Remember

Now that you are on your way to making your dream a reality there are a few things to keep in mind:

1. Dream building is an ongoing process.
2. Be prepared to adapt.
3. Stay current on trends.
4. Always invest in yourself and education.
5. Remember why you started.
6. Take time to relax.
7. Enjoy the ride.

Truly, living your dream is a great feeling. To see what you have always visualized turn into something tangible is remarkable. You are amazing!

Bonus Declarations

Speaking positively over your life can have incredible results. Use the following phrases to help stimulate the growth of your vision.

1. "I am a dream builder."
2. "I am surrounded by positivity."
3. "I am committed to creating a solid foundation for my dream."
4. "I will be proactive in protecting my dream."
5. "I am dedicated to sharing my dream with the world."
6. "I will manage my dream properly."
7. "My dream is a work in progress."

SHARE THE DREAM

"Your dream is meant to be shared."

-Miriam Jones

What you do is not meant to be kept secret. You are given special gifts and visions for a reason. Your contribution to the world is important. Please take a moment to think about ways that you can help others enjoy the fruits of your labor.

I hope you have enjoyed the content of this book. If it has been helpful for you, please share it with someone you love. Wishing you success and a life of fulfillment!

Live Life. Be Happy. Dream Big.

INDEX